I0469743

# Macro
# Photography
# Book 8

in

## "Quick Tips from a Pro Photographer"

series

*By Julia Harwood*

# Contents

1. Introduction
2. Understanding macro
3. Depth of field
4. Set-up for Macro
5. Flash
6. Home set-up for indoor shots
7. Tripod
8. Subjects to shoot
9. Composition
10. Special Thanks
11. Cheat Sheets

# Introduction

Macro photography is a specialized niche, but is also something we use in other parts of photography such as shooting flowers or abstracts.

I thought about doing the flowers book first but thought if you understand macro it will be much easier, even though you won't use macro for every flower.

Insects are one object that is often photographed in macro, giving us a bug's eye look at the world.

Other subjects are eyes, water drops, objects, inside of fruits, time pieces, fungi, colors, and as we mentioned before, flowers.

# So what exactly is macro?

Wikipedia says *"it is extreme close-up photography, usually of very small subjects, in which the size of the subject in the photograph is greater than life size, however in other uses it refers to a finished photograph of a subject at greater than life size."*

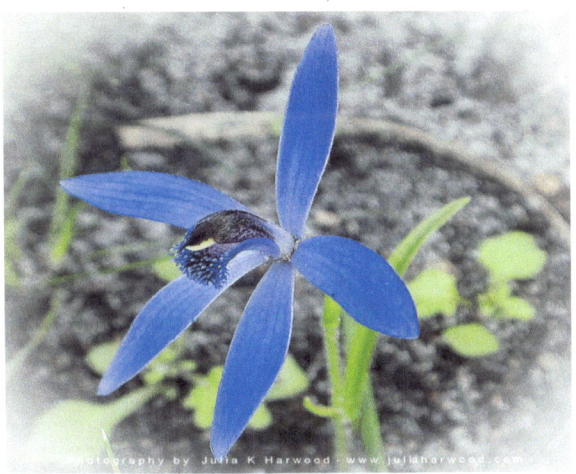

This flower is about the size of a 50 cent piece.

So most macro lenses will be at least 1:1, and we see this on a lot of zoom lenses that are sold as also macro, however a dedicated macro lens will usually give you greater magnification.

This doesn't mean you can't use the 1:1, for a lot of things this is all you need.

If you just occasionally want a closer image you can shoot through a magnifying glass and there is also a field called photomicrography that is images shot through a microscope.

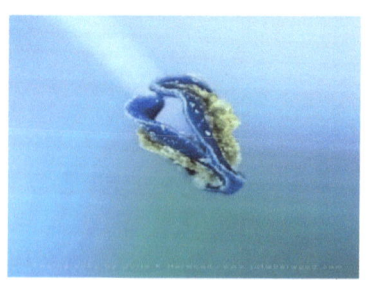

As this is a quick tips book I will not go into these specialist fields and will mainly be talking about images you can take with the camera and lenses you have.

So let's get started.

## Understanding Macro

There are some peculiarities that occur with macro that go against what we have been taught for general photography, so we will start with these.

Firstly, all movement is exaggerated. This means a tiny movement that wouldn't even register on a normal photo can ruin a macro shot.

To avoid this we need either a controlled environment or as calm a day as possible, if outside.
Around dawn is usually the stillest part of the day so is great for this.

The other setting that we know stops movement is a fast shutter speed. Sometimes we may need to increase the ISO to achieve this. Always try to work with a minimum shutter speed of 1/120 for still objects, faster if they are moving.

A tripod and a shutter release cable or using the timer function on the camera will also help not to introduce movement.

If using hand held, use a minimum shutter speed of 1/220 and hold your breath as you roll your finger onto the shutter button and then roll off again, to stop the camera registering the press of the shutter and creating movement in the image.

When you get a tripod it is worth considering your needs for close up and macro images. I have a Manfrotto tripod where the center stem unscrews, leaving just a small nib and the legs go right the way out so you can get down really low.

The other tripod I have has a reversible riser, so that you can take it out and put it in upside down so that your camera is close to the ground.

You can also try a Gorilla pod or tabletop tripod by Joby but make sure it is strong enough to hold your camera.

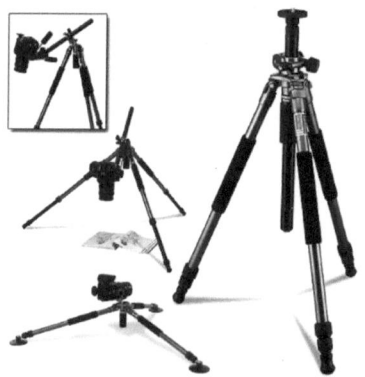

This is an example of a good macro tripod

# Depth of field

This is another anomaly when shooting in macro.

In ordinary photography f16 or higher would be a large depth of field, in macro it might get the whole insect in focus if the insect is quite small and if you use f2.8 you will probably only get a speck in focus.

Have a look at the following charts to get a greater understanding of how distance from subject and focal length of lens affect the depth of field and you will see why it becomes so crucial in macro photography.

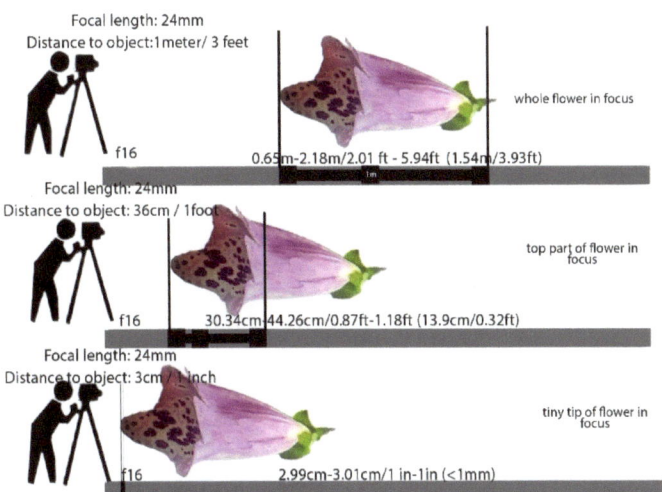

Focal length: 24mm
Distance to object:1meter/ 3 feet

f16

whole flower in focus

0.65m-2.18m/2.01 ft - 5.94ft (1.54m/3.93ft)

Focal length: 24mm
Distance to object: 36cm / 1foot

f16

top part of flower in focus

30.34cm-44.26cm/0.87ft-1.18ft (13.9cm/0.32ft)

Focal length: 24mm
Distance to object: 3cm / 1 inch

f16

tiny tip of flower in focus

2.99cm-3.01cm/1 in-1in (<1mm)

We can see here that as the distance to the subject becomes less, the depth of field also decreases dramatically even if the appature stays the same. This example uses f16, so if you used f2.8 and were really close to object you would only have a tiny section in focus.

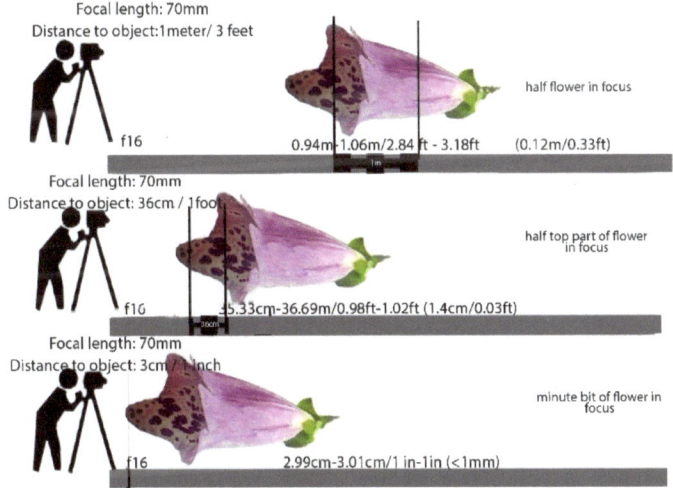

Focal length: 70mm
Distance to object:1meter/ 3 feet

f16

half flower in focus

0.94m-1.06m/2.84 ft - 3.18ft (0.12m/0.33ft)

Focal length: 70mm
Distance to object: 36cm / 1foot

f16

half top part of flower in focus

35.33cm-36.69m/0.98ft-1.02ft (1.4cm/0.03ft)

Focal length: 70mm
Distance to object: 3cm / 1 inch

f16

minute bit of flower in focus

2.99cm-3.01cm/1 in-1in (<1mm)

Going on from the previous chart if we change the focal length of the lens, we shorten the depth of field even more, so we need to use as wide an angle lens as we have, without going fisheye and as high an apature as we can. This is quite different to how we normally work as normally we would want a small f stop to blur the background, however the closer we are to an object (macro) the larger we need the f stop and the wider the focal length to maximize depth of field.

There is a trick we can use to maximize the depth of field and that is to shoot the insect or object side on, that way you have a larger plain of focus and at f12- f16 you should get the whole insect or small object in focus.

To get a high f stop we need plenty of light, we try not to increase the ISO if we can avoid it as we want to keep the image as clean and sharp as possible, so a good way to add extra light is with a ring flash. This puts the light right at the front of the lens where you need it. You can also use reflectors and a mirror often comes in handy.

Another way to increase depth of field is to stay back a bit and crop after, this is especially good if you have a high mega pixel camera. The closer we are to something, the smaller the depth of field, so by being a bit further away you enhance the depth of field. But don't stand further away and zoom in as this will make the depth of field even narrower (refer to previous chart).

One of the great things about macro is that you can shoot at any time of the day, even midday.
If you set the camera up to f16 and use the flash sync speed for the camera, usually around 1/200-1/250, check your manual, and have the flash on, then everything out of range of the flash will be dark, so it isolates the subject.

Another way to increase the depth of field is to focus stack multiple images.

To do this you need to use a tripod and a remote shutter release, you need to use manual focus and then leave everything the same as you very slowly move the focus ring, taking a photo at each step. Then you can load them into Photoshop and merge them into one image.

# Setup for Macro

Macro photography needs a little specialized gear. First you will need a macro lens. A lot of lenses, especially zoom lenses will say they are macro lenses and they do mostly up to 1:1, so they are a good place to start. As you get more into this area of photography you will want to look at more specialized equipment, starting from extension tubes, right up to high end macro lenses.

**Extension tubes**, these fit between the camera body and lens and it extends the length of the lens, it looks like a lens, but it has no glass. They are hollow tubes that enable you to move your lens away from the sensor in the camera thus allowing you to get closer to the subject and therefore a larger image of the subject.

There are two types, mechanical and electronic. Mechanical are the cheapest but you cannot auto focus unless your lens has aperture control rings.
Camera can handle aperture in AP mode or program mode. The image darkens as you close up the aperture making focusing harder.

An electronic one allows the camera and the lens to talk to each other so they can auto focus. They are sturdier than mechanical ones but they also cost more.

You can stack tubes to increase magnification.

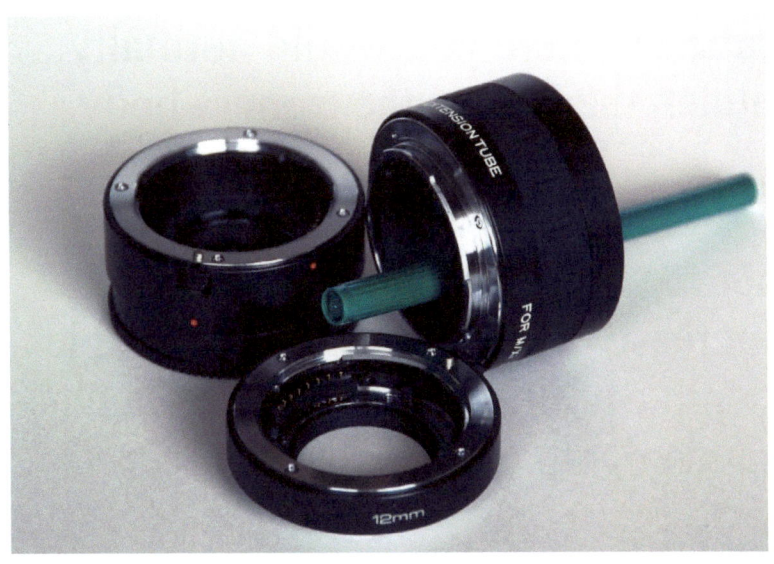

To work out what the magnification will be you take the length of the tube, say 30mm and divide it by the focal length of your lens, say you were using a 50mm lens. This would be 30/50 which equals 0.6 times magnification.

To fit extension tubes you turn off the camera, take the lens off, attach tube to lens, then attach extension tube to where you would normally attach the lens to the camera body.

When you use, if it is not electronic, set the focus to manual and then increase the ISO to get a reasonable depth of field, remember we want as much depth of field as possible.

These work best on small to medium focal length lenses, they aren't effective on a telephoto lens. Prime lenses are the best as they have the best optics,

For hand-held shots your minimum shutter speed should be 1/250.

This is a good start-out option.

**Close up Lenses**, are lenses that work like a filter, they screw on the front of your lens and act like a magnifying glass. This is the option to use if you are using a telephoto lens as this setup needs to be on a lens with a focal length of 80mm plus.

This option retains more light making focusing easier. You don't have to take your lens off to fit it, so don't risk damage to the sensor, especially in windy conditions.

*A note here, never take you lens off at the beach or in dusty, windy or wet conditions.*

The disadvantage is that you will have additional glass to shoot through, which can soften the image a little and it is more expensive than extension tubes, but it is cheaper than a macro lens.

To use this with no flash, set aperture to f16, this will give you a good depth of field for the object, but still blur the background. A focal length of 180-200mm works best. As you are using a longer focal length make sure you are far enough away from the subject to get a decent depth of field.

If you use a flash then the background will go black, this is a good way to eliminate distractions and help the object to stand out.

Telephoto lenses can be used in some instances, when it is safer to stand further back, like when don't want
that creepy crawly to bite you and it will also give you a better perspective as you won't get the distortion you can get from a wide angle lens. But be aware of the decreased depth of field from using a telephoto lens. So make sure you are a reasonable distance from the subject. For a 300mm lens if you were 3 m away you would have a depth of field of about 6cm at 6m you would have 24cm depth of field.

*Remember the minimum shutter speed hand-held is the inverse of the focal length, so if you are using a focal length of 300mm then the minimum hand-held is 1/300 sec.*

I find it is better to use a tripod if at all possible, you will get a sharper, cleaner image and it is easier to manually focus so you get a tack sharp image.

*Remember when using a tripod, turn IS (Image Stabilization) off and set camera to macro mode.*

**Teleconverters**, this is a secondary lens that is mounted between your lens and the camera body, thus moving the lens further from the sensor.

These are a cheaper alternative to a specialized lens and also work to give you a greater zoom as well.

The downside is that it cuts the light down and so affects your aperture. You also have to allow a little longer for the camera to focus and you can get some image degradation, but it still gives you a cleaner image than cropping, so worth considering.

**Reversing rings,** allow you to turn the lens around and this makes it into a macro lens, again be careful where you remove your lens, make sure you clean your sensor after using these. It allows the lens to act as a magnifying glass. You can buy adapters that enable you to do this.

Shorter focal length lenses give you greater magnification than long focal length lenses using this technique.

Some lenses allow you to stop down

the aperture in this setup and some don't so please do your research first to check you have a lens where you can stop down the aperture when the lens is reversed.

**Bellows**, these are usually only used on large or medium format cameras. These were used a lot in the old film days but are not used as much today.

**Macro lenses**, these are lenses that are designed exclusively for taking macro images and as such are capable of taking images with a much greater magnification and the lenses are usually fairly high quality glass and so are the most expensive of the options.

If you intend to focus on macro then they are a sound investment, however for the occasional shot they are too expensive.

The other thing most digital cameras have is a macro scene mode, so you can start out with this to give you an idea if you will like it or not.

Some even have settings for macro and super macro, so if your camera has these then utilize them.

For images of small flowers it is often best to shoot on the scene mode for flowers, this is a great way to get stated.

You can also try out a good quality point and shoot for these, so don't assume you need expensive equipment, start practicing with what you have

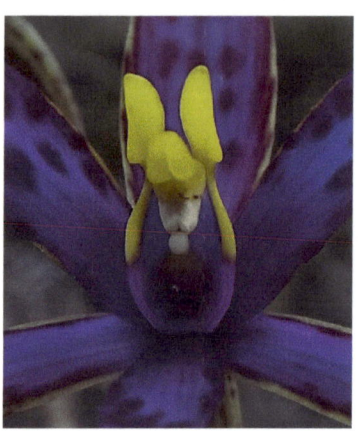

*This was shot on a small point and shoot on flower scene mode.*
*I shot a larger image and cropped it to get the larger depth of field.*

# Flash

The next thing I would suggest you invest in is a ring flash or a twin flash macro rig that places a flash either side and to the front of the camera, this gives even lighting at the front of the lens so you don't end up with a shadow from the lens falling on the subject. You can get away with other lighting set-ups if you are at home, but for out in the field this is the easiest solution.

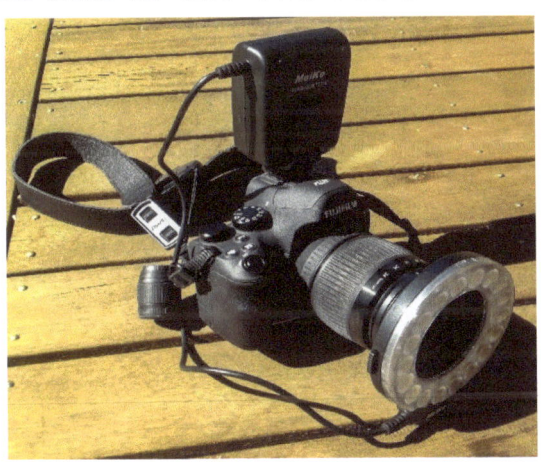

This is the ring flash on my camera.

There are also home made options you might want to try.

This link shows some of the home-made options that will work with the gear you already have.

http://orionmystery.blogspot.com.au/2010/12/more-macro-rigs.html

# Home Set-up for indoor shots

For home I would suggest you set up a macro photography area. Firstly I would set up a table that is a comfortable working height, either sitting or standing, It takes precision, time and patience to get good macro shots so making sure that you are comfortable is really important.

Also make sure there are no drafts or breezes blowing through the area as you want everything to be very still.

You can use window light, but also have some heavy drapes or dark fabric you can hang so that if the lighting is wrong you can set up your scene totally with light you are controlling.

I like to start off with as much ambient light as I can and then add any extra that I need.

I find a light-box is a great help. You can make these or buy them relatively cheaply online. http://digital-photography-school.com/how-to-make-a-inexpensive-light-tent/ or https://www.youtube.com/watch?v=OyxzC5kqbyw

I also find clamps are a great asset as you can place backgrounds, clamp lights or use as an extra set of hands.

You will need your tripod and camera as well.

# Tripod

Make sure you get a tripod that has a center pole that is in two pieces so that you can take the long part off and get the camera close to the ground. Also the tripod needs to have legs that go out flat. Another option is to get a tripod with a reversible center pole so that you can take it out and turn it around and then the camera is upside down and close to the ground or use a gorilla pod or similar.

Also remember to lock the mirror up (generally using live mode does this or refer to your manual), use a remote shutter release or if you don't have one use the timer function on your camera.

Focusing rails can help, as can a tilt shift lens.

# Subjects for Macro

The subjects for macro photography are endless and the great thing is it doesn't matter if you are housebound, only able to go as far as the backyard or able to travel the world. It is a medium that is available to everyone.

We have to start by looking beyond the surface. Instead of looking at an object, look at the individual parts that make up that object, now photograph each of these parts. This is a good way to take yourself from normal photography to macro photography.

Like with any photography, seeing and light are the two main elements.

Go out into your back yard and look in the bark of the trees, take shots of the bark, the buds, insects, flowers, and anything else you happen upon. Rust and peeling paint can create some great images too.

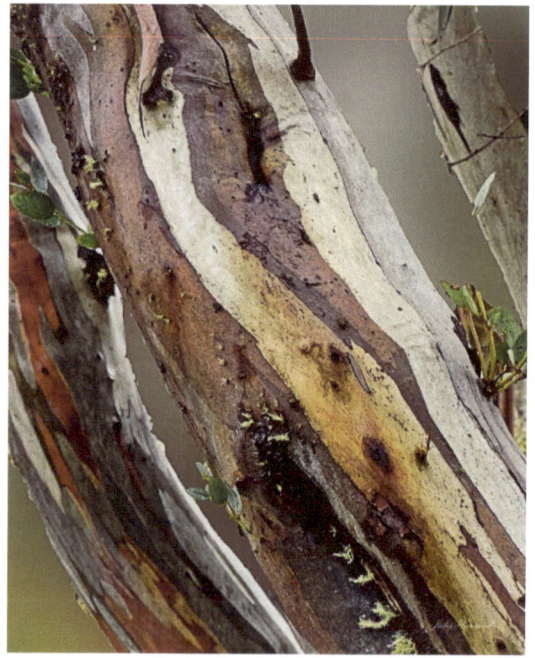

Bark of a tree

A mirror for shooting under things close to the ground or to add more light is a handy addition.

When you find something, say a flower, start by taking the whole flower, then just a leaf or a petal, the stem, the very center.
Are there any bugs, what about spider's webs.

Use a spray bottle and add some dew for another effect. To make the drops last longer, put glycerin in the spray bottle instead of water.

For really small objects use a syringe with a needle and drop the drops on one by one. This gives you great control.

Water drops make a great subject on their own.

Car or truck details, especially the engine and dashboard make great subjects.

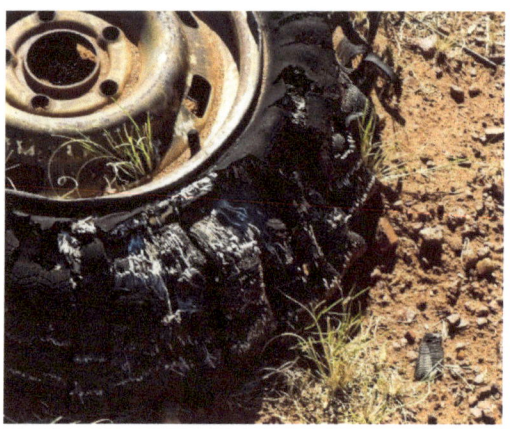

Try glass and foil for great reflections.

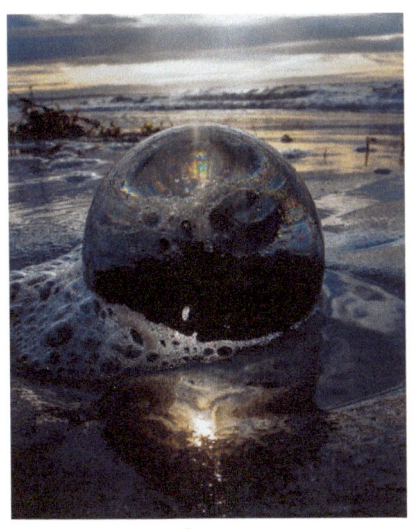

Invest in a glass sphere for some artistic images.

Don't forget the fruit bowl or the vegetable drawer.

Often slicing a piece of fruit will give you great detail, patterns and texture as well as you can play with the light to make them appear translucent.

Try fabric and tissues.

Macro is great for creating abstract images too, so let the artist in you out and see what you can create.

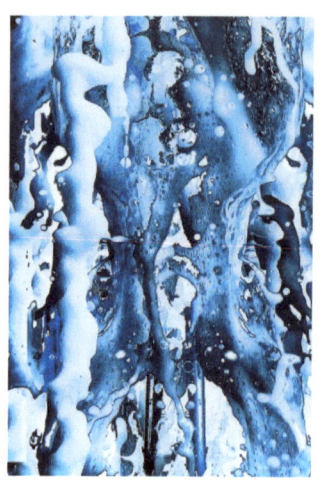

You will be amazed at the new world that will open up to you.

# Composition

This is often the most overlooked area of macro photography as we get so caught up in photographing this new world we forget the basics of composition.

You can get my Composition book here...
http://www.amazon.com/Composition-Quick-Tips-Photographer-Book-ebook/dp/B00WXH49AU

A lot of intricate detail fits the spiral rule so look out for this one.

Try to add depth to your image with layers and remember patterns, colors and texture are important composition elements.

# Focus

Focusing becomes difficult as we are so close to the object and as the depth of field is so limited we need to get the focus spot on so now is the time to start practicing your manual focus.

Even though this is a skill we don't use much in modern photography you will be amazed at the clarity and sharpness of your images when you do.

Set your focus to spot metering.

Try to get side on to the object or insect so that you have the maximum amount of the object in the focal plane.

This is an article that has diagrams to give you a visual perspective on how the depth of field changes in macro photography.
http://macroshooting.com/DepthofField.htm

We will also talk about focus stacking. This is where we take a series of images of the same object with everything staying exactly the same except for where we focus. We need at least three shots, one at the front, one in the middle and one towards the back.

The more shots you take the more detail you get, but the more processing power you will need in your computer to process the images.

Another tool that is helpful here is a macro focusing rail.
You use these so that you focus the camera by moving it backwards and forwards rather than focusing with the focus ring. It allows a closer more accurate focusing but takes a lot of time and patience.

When looking for rails look for ones that have a solid build, has knobs for fine adjustment and the ability to lock the rail positions are all important.

You can generally only use this on images you take inside so that you can control all the external factors and it has to be objects that don't move.

Some people put insects to sleep by lowering their body temperature, while it is something I don't do, if you want more information on this then have a look at my book called, "Quick Tips from a Pro Photographer book 5 Photographing Animals". You can get it here http://amzn.to/1dA3EuZ it is available as an e-book or a paperback.

A tilt shift lens is another option.

# Get down to Subject's Level

This is why I suggested a table as it can get hard on our back and knees if we are kneeling down all the time. If you are outside take a picnic blanket or a light weight tarp so you can put it on the ground and then lay down on it. This will protect you from insect bites, poison bushes and the dirt itself. It is a safety measure as much as anything.

If you are able to get a light colored tarp then you can also use it as a reflector.

One of the things that entices us about macro images is that we are seeing things from a perspective that we don't often get to see, so getting down to the level of the object is very important.

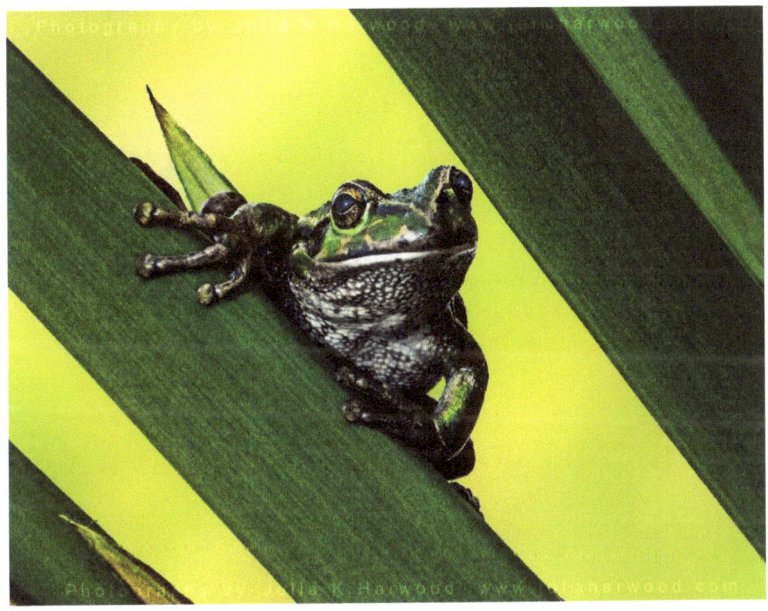

If it is something you can pick up and bring inside then do that, but also remember that inside you are going to have to create a background whereas out in nature one is provided for you.

I always carry a piece of black card, then if the background is distracting or my subject is blending in with it, I can place the black card behind it and isolate it beautifully, making the image all about the object.

This means you have to rely on the object for the composition.

How do you get close to a flighty subject?
The morning is always best as there is less breeze and the insects are usually sluggish until they warm up.

With dragonflies if you approach them slowly from side on you can get closer than coming from in front or behind. This technique takes time, but you take a step, allow yourself to sway slightly from side to side and then take another step. The dragonfly tends to forget you are there, but remember small steps and gentle movements.

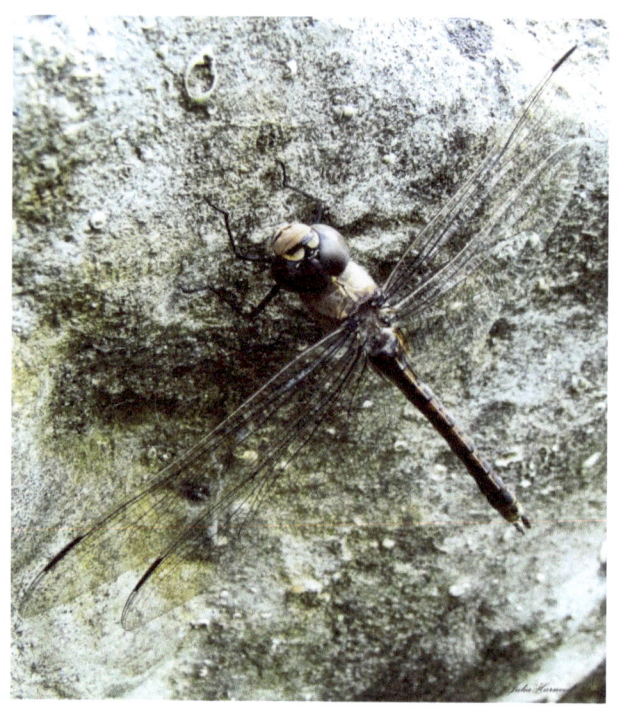

Bees are great, they don't scare easy so if they are feeding they will stay until they have finished so they are a good one to practice on, unless you are allergic to bees, then stay well away:)

With bees you can pre-focus on the flower and then wait for the bee to arrive.

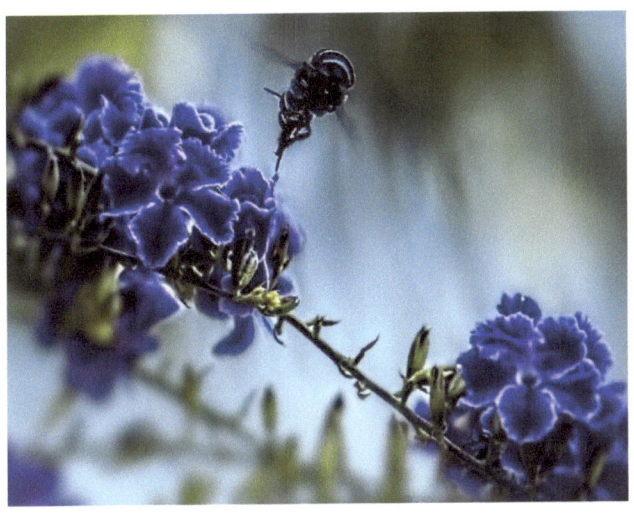

Spiders are a great one to practice on as they don't move fast and you can get some of their web as well.

# Special Thanks

I would like to make a special mention of a few people who without their support this series would not be possible. Firstly to my Proof Reader, Cathy Longley, no matter how sick you were you still managed to get these done, thank you so much. The to all my supporters on Pozible but most especially Angela Chan, as without her financial backing this project would not have been possible and finally to my wonderful husband Colin, who put up with me spending so many hours on the computer. I hope these help you on your photographic journey.

You can also follow me on my website at Photography by Julia K Harwood
http://www.juliaharwood.com/

For all your gift needs
http://www.redbubble.com/people/juliakharwood/portfolio
To follow me on G+
http://plus.google.com/+JuliaHarwood

To follow on FB
http://m.facebook.com/Photography.by.Julia.K.Harwood

To view a gallery of my images
http://photographybyjuliakharwood.shootproof.com/juliaharwood

# Cheat Sheet

Use at least 1/120 sec to eliminate movement.

Tripod, shutter release (timer), IS off, Live view (locks mirror)

Ring flash

Use highest f stop for max depth of field.

Increase ISO if you need to to get the settings right.

Adding flash helps.

F16 at 1/200 or 1/250 (your flash sync speed) will give a black background.

Take a spray bottle of water with glycerin in it to create water drops

**Focus: Depth of field:**
Use a wide angle, f16, 1 foot or 36cm = 1/3 foot or 14cm.

The closer you get the higher f stop you need.

Shoot so the largest plain of the object is facing you if you want maximum depth of field. (i.e. Side on to a praying mantis).

Tripod with *IS (image stabilization) off.*

Ring flash or side lights

Pre focus if shooting insects and wait for them to come to the focus area.

Get down to subjects level.

Take a point and shoot with you as well and experiment with flower or macro mode.

You can also get macro lenses for your smart phones that are fun to play with.

Remember Composition

**Subjects to shoot**

Bark, leaves, flower, roots

Parts of objects

Rust, old paint

Reflections, glass, foil

Glass ball

Insects, spiders, spiders web

Water drops

Car or truck details